SCIENCE PROJECT IDEAS

Science Project Ideas About

RAIN

Robert Gardner

Enslow Publishers, Inc.

44 Fadem Road	PO Box 38
Box 699	Aldershot
Springfield, NJ 07081	Hants GU12 6BP
USA	UK

Library of Congress Cataloging-in-Publication Data

Gardner, Robert, 1929–
    Science project ideas about rain / Robert Gardner.
       p. cm.—(Science project ideas)
    Includes bibliographical references and index.
    Summary: Uses experiments to illustrate the properties of rain as
    well as the reasons that water is such an important part of life.
    ISBN 0-89490-843-X
    1. Rain and rainfall—Experiments—Juvenile literature.
    2. Clouds—Experiments—Juvenile literature. [1. Rain and rainfall—
Experiments. 2. Clouds—Experiments. 3. Experiments.]
    I. Title. II. Series: Gardner, Robert, 1929– Science project ideas.
    QC924.7.G37 1997
    551.57'7'078—DC20   96-42411
                                                             CIP
                                                             AC

Printed in the United States of America

10 9 8 7 6 5 4 3 2 1

Illustration Credits: Jacob Katari

Photo Credits: © Corel Corporation, pp. 42, 43.

Cover Photo: Jerry McCrea

CONTENTS

INTRODUCTION

In this book you will find experiments about rain and its relatives—clouds, fog, and snow. The experiments use simple everyday materials you can find at home or at school.

The book will help you to work the way real scientists do. You will be answering questions by doing experiments to understand basic scientific principles.

Most of the experiments will provide detailed guidance. But some of them will raise questions and ask you to make up your own experiments to answer them. This is the kind of experiment that could be a particularly good start for a science fair project. Such experiments are marked with an asterisk(*).

Please note: **If an experiment uses anything that has a potential for danger, you will be asked to work with an adult.** *Please do so! The purpose of this teamwork is to prevent you from being hurt. Science Project Ideas About Rain can open science's door for you—and make you happy to see a rainy day!*

MEASUREMENT ABBREVIATIONS			
centimeter	cm	kilometers per hour	kph
cubic kilometer	cu km	liter	l
cubic meter	cu m	meter	m
cubic millimeter	cu mm	miles per hour	mph
foot	ft	millimeter	mm
gram	g	tablespoon	tbsp
inch	in	teaspoon	tsp
kilometer	km		

The thirsty earth soaks up the rain,
And drinks, and gapes for drink again.

(Abraham Cowley)

1

RAIN AND THE WATER CYCLE

Without water we cannot live, and that water comes to us first as rain. Rain seeps into soil and nurtures the plants that we and other animals eat. It provides the water that fills our wells, lakes, and ponds. Rain that drains away into rivers serves as a highway for ships, water for irrigation, and energy to make electric power.

Water, the basis of life, is also the lifeblood of agriculture and industry.

Every bushel of corn requires about 13,000 liters of water. A similar amount of rain is needed to produce a pound of beef; and 450 liters (120 gallons) are needed for each egg you eat. To process one ton of wood pulp, 225,000 liters of water are used; distilling 15 liters of gasoline requires more than 150 liters of water; and 150,000 liters of water are needed to manufacture one automobile. An average American uses more than 450 liters of water every day.

Each day more than a quadrillion liters of rain fall on the earth. In a single year, 491 quadrillion liters (130 quadrillion gallons) of rain fall on the earth. (A quadrillion is a one followed by 15 zeros.) A little more than one fifth of that rain falls on land. Spread evenly over the earth, the total rainfall (if it didn't evaporate) would cover the earth with a layer of water almost one meter (38 inches) deep. But, rain does not fall evenly over the earth's surface. In some places, a lot of rain falls, in other places it seldom rains. For example, on Mount Waialeala in Hawaii, 11.7 meters (460 inches) of rain fall each year. At Kharga Oasis in Egypt, only a trace of rain is detected.

MEASURING RAINFALL

To do this experiment you will need:

- ✔ large container with straight sides such as a coffee can or a large peanut butter jar
- ✔ narrow transparent container with straight sides such as an olive jar
- ✔ ruler
- ✔ masking tape
- ✔ stake
- ✔ nail
- ✔ string or wire

Rain is usually measured in millimeters (mm) or inches (in). You can make a simple rain gauge that will allow you to measure how much rain falls during a storm. Any large container with straight sides can be used to collect rain. A coffee can or a large peanut butter jar works well. Why should you NOT use a jar with a mouth that is narrower than the rest of the jar?

Rainfalls often produce less than 25 mm (1 in) of rain. Small amounts of rain are difficult to measure accurately in a large container. You can measure more accurately by pouring any water you collect into a narrower transparent container with straight sides, such as the kind of jar that olives come in. To put measurements

FIGURE 1

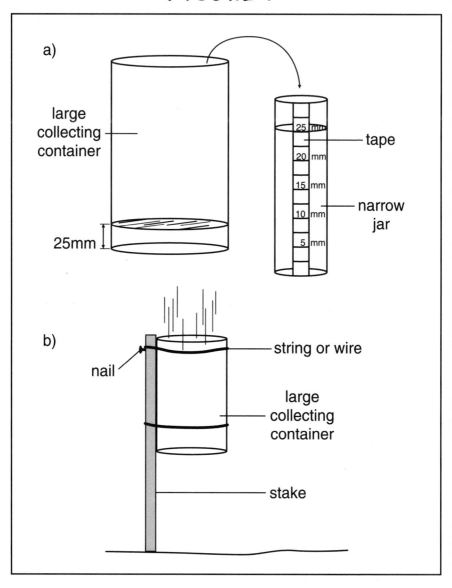

a) A large container with 25 mm (1.0 in) of water is shown. The water is poured into a narrow container so that rainfall can be measured more accurately.

b) Before a rain, tie the large collecting container to a vertical stake in an open area.

on the narrow jar, pour water into the large container until the water is exactly 25 mm (1.0 in) deep. Then pour that water into the narrow jar. Place a strip of masking tape along the side of the narrow jar. Mark the height of the water on the tape and label it 25 mm (1.0 in). Divide the distance from the mark to the bottom of the jar into ten equal spaces (see Figure 1a). Each line corresponds to 2.5 mm (0.1 in) of rain. If the jar holds more than 25 mm of water, you can continue to mark the tape to the top of the jar with equally-spaced lines. How can you measure more than 25 mm of rain if the smaller jar will hold no more than 25 mm of rain?

Before the next rain falls, tie the large, empty container to the top of a stake in an open area far from trees, bushes, and buildings, as shown in Figure 1b. Why should you measure the rain you've collected as soon as possible after the rain stops?

Measure and record rainfall over the course of several years or more. Is there one time of the year when more rain falls? Is there a period during which little rain falls? What is the total precipitation (rainfall + melted snowfall) for an entire year. (See Experiment 4.1 to find out how to convert inches of snowfall to depth of rain.)

NORMAL ANNUAL PRECIPITATION FOR A NUMBER OF U.S. CITIES TO NEAREST MILLIMETER (MM) OR INCH.

LOCATION	PRECIPITATION mm (inches)	LOCATION	PRECIPITATION mm (inches)
Mobile, AL	1,626 (64)	Duluth, MN	762 (30)
Anchorage, AK	406 (16)	Jackson, MS	1,397 (55)
Phoenix, AZ	203 (8)	Kansas City, MO	965 (38)
Little Rock, AR	1,829 (72)	Helena, MT	305 (12)
Los Angeles, CA	381 (15)	Omaha, NB	762 (30)
San Francisco, CA	508 (20)	Reno, NV	203 (8)
Denver, CO	381 (15)	Atlantic City, NJ	1,016 (40)
Hartford, CT	1,118 (44)	Albany, NY	914 (36)
Wilmington, DE	1,041 (41)	Raleigh, NC	1,041 (41)
Washington, D.C.	991 (39)	Bismarck, ND	381 (15)
Jacksonville, FL	1,295 (51)	Cleveland, OH	940 (37)
Miami, FL	1,422 (56)	Portland, OR	914 (36)
Atlanta, GA	1,295 (51)	Philadelphia, PA	1,041 (41)
Honolulu, HI	559 (22)	Providence, RI	1,168 (46)
Boise, ID	305 (12)	Charleston, SC	1,321 (52)
Chicago, IL	914 (36)	Rapid City, SD	432 (17)
Indianapolis, IN	1,016 (40)	Memphis, TN	1,321 (52)
Des Moines, IA	838 (33)	Houston, TX	1,168 (46)
Lexington, KY	1,143 (45)	Burlington, VT	864 (34)
New Orleans, LA	1,575 (62)	Richmond, VA	1,092 (43)
Portland, ME	1,041 (41)	Seattle-Tacoma, WA	940 (37)
Baltimore, MD	1,067 (42)	Milwaukee, WI	838 (33)
Boston, MA	1,067 (42)	Lander, WY	330 (13)
Detroit, MI	838 (33)		

Table 1 shows the annual precipitation (rainfall + melted snowfall) at a number of United States weather stations. How does your measurement of annual precipitation compare with that given for the weather station in Table 1 that is nearest to you?

The Water Cycle

Rain is but one part of the water cycle, a cycle that keeps the earth's water circulating. A third of the rain that falls on land runs off into rivers. The rivers carry water back to the ocean from which most of it came. The water in lakes, ponds, rivers, and oceans (which contain more than 95 percent of the earth's water) is constantly evaporating. During evaporation, water changes from a liquid to a gas. The gaseous water becomes mixed with the other components of air— mostly nitrogen and oxygen.

Evaporation occurs throughout the world. But evaporation is greatest from warm ocean water near the equator. The moist air over the equator rises and is carried northward and southward by winds. As the moist air cools, gaseous water changes back to a liquid. The change from gas to liquid is called condensation. We say the gas condenses to a

FIGURE 2

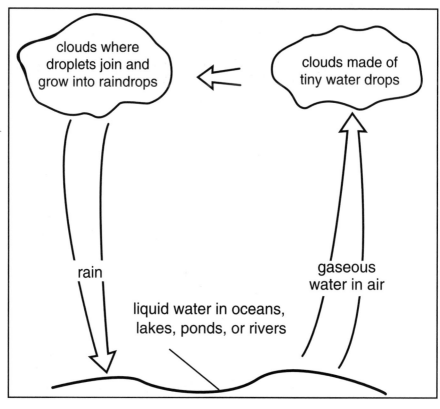

In the water cycle, water evaporates into the atmosphere as a gas. When the gaseous water cools, it condenses into tiny droplets. These droplets join to form larger drops that fall to the earth as rain.

liquid. At first, the condensed droplets are tiny. They remain suspended in the air as clouds. Under certain conditions, the droplets join together to form larger drops that fall to the earth as rain. This completes the water cycle, which is shown in Figure 2.

Experiment 1.2

EVAPORATING WATER

To do this experiment you will need:

- ✔ two saucers
- ✔ drinking glass
- ✔ water
- ✔ file cards

- ✔ salt
- ✔ teaspoon
- ✔ magnifying glass

Place a saucer in a warm place in your house. Fill a drinking glass about halfway with water. Pour a small amount of the water onto the saucer. On a card write: "plain water." Place the card beside the saucer.

Add 2 tsp of salt to the water that remains in the glass. Stir until the salt dissolves. Place another saucer near the first one. Pour the same amount of the salty water onto this second saucer. On another card write: "salt water." Place this card beside the second saucer.

Watch these two saucers over the next few hours and into the next day or two. What happens to the amount of water that remains in the saucers? How can you explain what happens? Could you tell which saucer contained the salty water even if the cards beside the saucers were lost?

Use a magnifying glass to look closely at the salt crystals on the saucer that held the salt water. What is the shape of these crystals?

DID YOU KNOW. . .?

Seawater is 3.5 percent salt—mostly sodium chloride, the same salt you put on food. This means the oceans hold about 46 quadrillion metric tons of salt.

Experiment *1.3

A Model of the Water Cycle

To do this experiment you will need:

- ✔ an ADULT
- ✔ water
- ✔ stove or hot plate
- ✔ glass saucepan or coffe pot
- ✔ dish
- ✔ ice cubes

The water that evaporated in Experiment 1.2 became mixed with the air in the room. It added moisture to the air, but it probably did not condense and fall as rain. To see a model of the complete water cycle, **ASK AN ADULT** to help you heat some water in a glass saucepan or coffee pot on a stove or hot plate. Place a dish with some ice cubes in it over the top of the saucepan or coffee pot, as shown in Figure 3. Heat the water until it is hot but not boiling. You will see water that has evaporated begin to condense on the bottom of the cold saucer.

What happens as the drops of condensed water grow larger by joining with one another?

In this model of the water cycle, what corresponds to the ocean? What represents a cloud? Where is the rain in this model?

FIGURE 3

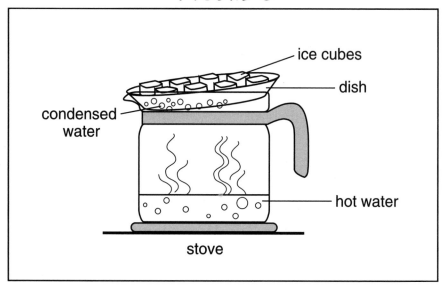

A model of the water cycle can be made quite easily.

Experiment *1.4

FACTORS THAT AFFECT EVAPORATION

To do this experiment you will need:

- ✔ teaspoon
- ✔ water
- ✔ two identical saucers
- ✔ cool and warm open, dry places, not in the wind
- ✔ upright test tube or vial
- ✔ tablespoon
- ✔ paper towels
- ✔ clothespins
- ✔ fan

For water to enter the air, form clouds, and fall back to earth as rain, it must first evaporate. What are some of the things that might make water evaporate faster? You might guess that the temperature of the water would be important. Can you think of other factors?

Let's begin by looking at the effect of temperature. Place exactly 1 tsp of water on each of two identical saucers. Place one saucer in a cool, dry place. Place the other in a warm, dry place. In which place does the water evaporate faster? How does temperature affect evaporation?

To test the effect of temperature on evaporation in another way, wet two paper towels in water. Spread out both towels. Hang one on a line in a warm dry area. Hang the other in a cool dry place. Which towel dries faster?

Does the amount of surface exposed to the air affect evaporation? To find out, put a saucer and an upright test tube or vial side by side in a warm dry place. Put exactly 2 tbsp of water in the saucer. Put the same amount in the test tube or vial. In which container does the water have more surface exposed to the air? From which container does all the water evaporate first? How does the amount of surface exposed to the air affect the rate of evaporation?

Do you think that wind affects the rate at which water evaporates? To find out, wet two paper towels in water. Spread out the towels. Hang one in a quiet area where no air is moving. Hang the other in front of a fan. Which towel dries faster? Does wind affect the rate at which evaporation occurs?

The World's Moving Water

Each year, 491 quadrillion liters (130 quadrillion gallons) of water fall to the earth as rain. That rain comes from the same volume of water that evaporates into the air every year. The volume of water that evaporates from the ocean each year is 423 quadrillion liters (112 quadrillion gallons); the volume evaporated each year from land, lakes, ponds, and rivers is 68 quadrillion liters (18 quadrillion gallons). But the volume of rain that falls on land is 108 quadrillion liters (29 quadrillion gallons). Only 383 quadrillion liters (101 quadrillion gallons) fall back into the oceans (see Table 2). What happens to the

TABLE 2

THE WORLD'S WATER—EVAPORATION AND RAINFALL

WATER EVAPORATED EACH YEAR (in quadrillion liters)		
From oceans	*From land, lakes and rivers*	*Total*
423	68	491

WATER THAT FALLS AS RAIN EACH YEAR (in quadrillion liters)		
To oceans	*To land, lakes and rivers*	*Total*
383	108	491

40 quadrillion liters (11 quadrillion gallons) of water that fall onto land but do not evaporate from the land?

The extra 40 quadrillion liters of water that fall on the continents (land) each year flow over land (as rivers) and through the land to lakes and rivers. Eventually it runs back into the ocean.

The 491 quadrillion liters of water that evaporate and fall as rain each year are a small portion (less than 0.04 percent; 4/10,000) of the world's total water. Table 3 shows where the world's water is found.

Underground Water (Aquifers)

Only half of the 8,340,000 cu km of underground water can be used. The rest is too far below the surface of the earth. Still, these 4,170,000 cu km provide water for more than half the world's population.

These underground sources of water are called aquifers. They are replenished by rain that seeps through the soil. Eventually, the draining rainwater reaches porous rock or gravel that rests on a thick bedrock through which water cannot pass. Once the spaces between the rock and gravel are filled with water, the space is said to be saturated. The top of this saturated zone is called the water table.

WHERE THE WORLD'S WATER IS LOCATED

LOCATION	AMOUNT (in cubic kilometers)*
Oceans	1,321,890,000
Polar ice caps	37,530,000
Underground (aquifers)	8,340,000
Lakes and ponds	125,100
Soil	66,720
Atmosphere (water vapor)	12,927
Rivers	1,251

* A cubic kilometer (cu km) is one trillion liters or 264 billion gallons.

Where land lies beneath the water table, we have a lake or pond.

In some regions, water is obtained from wells. The wells must be dug or drilled until they reach below the water table. During a drought (a long time during which little or no rain falls), water may be pumped from an aquifer faster than water reaches it. As a result, the water table may be lowered considerably. If the water table falls below the depth to which the wells have been dug or drilled, water cannot be pumped from the wells. We say the wells have "gone dry." Only rain can bring the aquifer's water table back to its previous level.

In some parts of the world, including many parts of the United States, water is being drawn from aquifers faster than it is being replaced by rainwater. To reach these aquifers, wells are being drilled ever deeper. Perhaps when bedrock is reached, people will realize that the earth's water is not unlimited.

Experiment *1.5

A Model Aquifer

To do this experiment you will need:

✔ aquarium, glass bowl, or plastic box	✔ transparent drinking straws
✔ modeling clay	✔ food coloring
✔ sand or gravel	✔ pail of water
	✔ spray or sprinkling can

You can build a model of an aquifer by covering the bottom of an aquarium, glass bowl, or plastic box with a layer of modeling clay. The clay represents the bedrock beneath the soil. Water cannot pass through it. Next, add sand or gravel, to represent soil. Vary the height of the soil to make hills and valleys. Also, use several transparent drinking straws to "drill" shallow and deep "wells" in the soil, as shown in Figure 4. The lowest soil elevation should be at least 2 cm (1 in) above the "bedrock." If you'd like, you can spread some top soil over the sand or gravel to make a more realistic model of farmland.

FIGURE 4

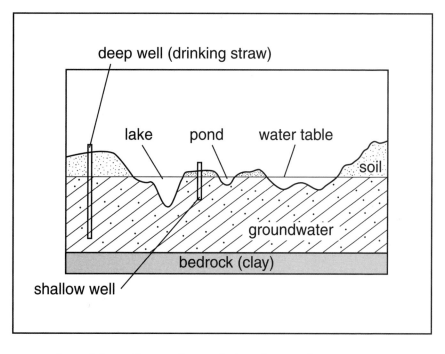

A model aquifer can be made in a large, clear container.

Add some food coloring to a pail of water and let "rain" fall on the model by spraying or sprinkling the colored water onto the soil. Observe how the water seeps in. The glass or plastic wall should provide a good side view of the soil.

After a while, you will see a "water table" beginning to rise above the "bedrock." What happens to the water table as more water is added? Can you see "ponds" forming? Which wells reach below the water table?

To see what happens during a drought, stop adding water for a few days. What happens to the water table? How does the changing water table affect lakes and wells? Now, add more "rain" and see how it affects your model aquifer.

What would you have to do to add a "pond" to your model? Can you build two lakes connected by a river? If you succeed, what causes water to flow in the river?

Experiment *1.6

THE SIZE OF RAINDROPS

To do this experiment you will need:

✔ baking pan and cover	✔ waxed paper
✔ baking flour	✔ tape
✔ rain	✔ cardboard
✔ tweezers	✔ coffee can
✔ paper	✔ nylon stocking
✔ ruler	✔ rubber band
✔ magnifying glass	✔ powdered sugar

How big is a raindrop? That was a question asked more than a century ago by W. A. Bentley, a farmer from Jericho, Vermont. You can do experiments similar to his and find the size of raindrops for yourself.

Fill a baking pan with at least 2.5 cm (1 in) of flour. Cover the pan and carry it out into an open area where rain is falling. **DO NOT GO OUTSIDE DURING A THUNDERSTORM!** Remove the cover for a few seconds so that raindrops can fall into the flour. The rain will form tiny pellets when they collide with the flour. Cover the pan again and take it inside.

FIGURE 5

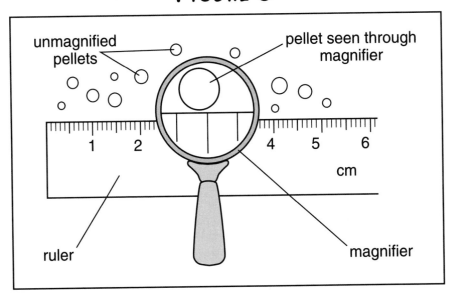

You can measure the diameter of a raindrop. The ruler shown is a centimeter (cm) ruler. Each centimeter is divided into 10 millimeters (mm). One in=2.54 cm, so a millimeter is about 0.04 (4/100) in.

Allow at least an hour for the pellets to dry. Then use tweezers to remove a few dry pellets from the pan. Place the pellets on a clean piece of paper. With a ruler and a magnifier estimate the width of each pellet (probably in mm), as shown in Figure 5. Were the raindrops all the same size? If not, what were the smallest and largest drops that fell into the flour?

You can determine the volume of the drops (pellets) as well. The volume of a drop is approximately equal to half the width cubed. That is:

Volume=1/2 (width)^3 or
Volume=1/2 (width x width x width)

For example, if the width of a pellet is 2 mm, its volume is approximately:

Volume=1/2 x (2 mm)^3 =
1/2 x (2 mm x 2 mm x 2 mm)=
1/2 x 8 cubic millimeters (cu mm)=4 cu mm

What was the volume of the largest raindrop you collected? What was the volume of your smallest raindrop?

In a gentle rain where very fine drops are drifting to the ground, you can collect the droplets on a piece of waxed paper taped to a sheet of cardboard (Figure 6). Be sure the drops do not spatter when they land! These drops will form hemispheres (a ball cut in half) on the waxed paper.

Again, you can take the drops to a covered place, preferably one that is outside where the drops will not evaporate very fast. Measure their widths with a ruler and magnifier. What is the largest drop you can find? What is the smallest drop you can find?

Here, because you are measuring hemispheres (half of a sphere), the volume is

approximately one quarter of the width cubed.
That is:

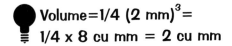 Volume=1/4 (width)^3 or
Volume=1/4 (width x width x width)

For example, if the width of a hemisphere is 2 mm, its volume is:

Volume=1/4 (2 mm)^3=
1/4 x 8 cu mm = 2 cu mm

Here is still another method for measuring the size of raindrops. It was unknown to Bentley because nylon had not been invented when he did his work. Cover the open top of an

FIGURE 6

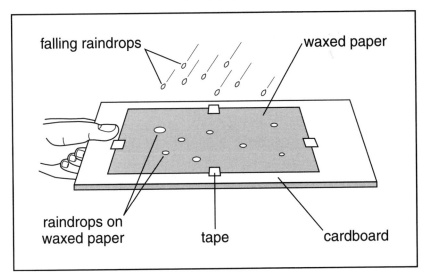

Very small raindrops can be collected on waxed paper.

empty coffee can with a piece of nylon stocking. Hold the nylon in place with a rubber band stretched around the can near its top. Sprinkle a thin layer of powdered sugar on the nylon. Cover the sugar-coated nylon with a sheet of cardboard and take it outside into the rain. Remove the cardboard cover for a couple of seconds so that a few raindrops can fall through the sugar and into the can. The drops will dissolve the sugar leaving measurable circles as they pass through the nylon. Use a ruler and magnifier to measure the diameter of the circles. (A circle's diameter is the width or distance across the circle.) How large were the raindrops? What were their volumes?

As your skill in collecting and measuring raindrops improves, you can carry out a number of experiments to answer these and other questions:

- *Does the average size of the raindrops change as a storm progresses?*

- *Are the raindrops that fall in a summer rain larger than those that fall in the winter?*

- *Are the raindrops that fall during a brief shower larger than those that fall in a long, steady rain?*

- *How many average-size raindrops are in a snowflake? in a hailstone?*

Experiment *1.7

THE SHAPE OF RAINDROPS

To do this experiment you will need:

- ✔ vacuum cleaner that will blow air
- ✔ food coloring
- ✔ water
- ✔ small glass
- ✔ eyedropper
- ✔ Ping-Pong ball

When raindrops fall in still air, they fall at a steady speed. This steady speed is called the terminal velocity of the raindrops. As you might guess, big drops have a larger terminal velocity than small drops. But all drops have a terminal velocity. In a wind tunnel, air can be directed upward until it keeps raindrops in place. The air will move by the drop at the same speed that the drop would fall through the air at its terminal velocity. You have experienced something similar when you ride a bike. Riding your bike at 19 kph (12 mph) through still air provides the same movement of air against your face as does a 19-kph (12-mph) wind when you stand still.

Artists often draw tear-shaped raindrops, but what is the actual shape of a raindrop? If you have a vacuum cleaner that will blow air, as well as draw air into the machine, you can investigate the shape of raindrops. The air stream from the vacuum cleaner will take the place of a much more expensive wind tunnel.

Add a drop or two of food coloring to some water in a small glass. Use an eyedropper to place a drop of the colored water in an upward directed stream of air from the vacuum cleaner. To help you locate the stream, place a Ping-Pong ball in the air stream. The ball will remain in the center of the flowing air. You will have to experiment until you find a place where the drops fall very slowly. The drops you see appear the same as do raindrops falling at a steady speed through air. What is the shape of falling raindrops?

SPLASHING RAINDROPS

To do this experiment you will need:

- ✔ eyedropper
- ✔ glassful of water
- ✔ food coloring
- ✔ ruler
- ✔ camera (optional)
- ✔ fast black-and-white film (optional)
- ✔ a friend

- ✔ white paper
- ✔ different surfaces; e.g., wood, aluminum, foil, various soils, concrete
- ✔ waxed paper
- ✔ tape
- ✔ cardboard
- ✔ books or blocks

You have probably watched raindrops falling into a pond or puddle. Each raindrop makes a ring of small waves that travel outward in circles. The centers of these circles mark the place where the drop struck the water. Watch a drop closely as it falls into water. You may be able to see a jet of water rise up above the point where the drop lands.

To see such a jet, use an eyedropper to release a drop into a glassful of water. Adding food coloring to the water will help you see it.

How far do the drops have to fall before they produce jets? It all takes place so fast that you won't be able to see all that happens, but you can see the jets and the tiny drop that breaks off from the top of the jet. If you have a good camera, you may be able to take pictures of what happens. With fast black-and-white film and good lighting, have a friend release the drops while you take pictures. It will take a large number of photos to capture the progress of the event, but you will enjoy seeing what happens if you are successful. It is a good idea to practice with an empty camera before you actually start taking photographs. After a few trials, you will be able to judge the time for the drop to reach the water after it is released.

You can also see what happens to raindrops that fall on dry surfaces. Tape a sheet of white paper to a flat surface. Let drops of colored water fall from an eyedropper onto the paper. Hold the eyedropper at different heights above the paper—1 cm, 5 cm, 15 cm, 30 cm, 60 cm, 90 cm, and higher (0.5 in, 2 in, 6 in, 1 ft, 2 ft, 3 ft, and higher). How does the splash pattern made when the drop lands change as the height increases? Do you reach a height after which the pattern does not change?

Does the kind of surface the drop lands on affect the splash pattern? To find out, you can let the drops fall on wood, aluminum foil, various soils, concrete, and other kinds of material. If possible, try letting the drops fall on waxed paper. Because waxed paper repels water, you might expect the splash pattern to be different. Try to predict what the pattern will be like. Then check your prediction. Is the pattern what you expected it would be?

Place several sheets of paper end to end on a flat surface (Figure 7). Then see what happens to the splash pattern if the drop is moving sideways when you release it. This is the way

FIGURE 7

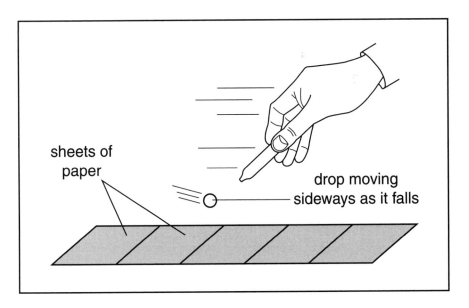

sheets of paper

drop moving sideways as it falls

What does the splash pattern look like if a drop is moving sideways when it lands?

raindrops land if they are driven by a wind as they fall. How does the pattern change if you increase the speed at which the eyedropper is moving when you release the drop?

Suppose the drops fall on a "hill" (Figure 8) instead of a flat surface. Do you think this will affect the splash pattern? To find out, tape some paper to a sheet of cardboard. Rest one end of the cardboard on some books or blocks of some kind so that the paper is inclined (tilted) instead of flat. Is the splash pattern different on a hill than on a flat surface? Try to predict what will happen to the splash pattern if you make the hill steeper. Try to predict what will happen if you make it less steep. Test your predictions. Are the patterns what you expected them to be?

DID YOU KNOW. . .?

Farmers plow around hills rather than up and down them to prevent the soil from being washed away in rainstorms. The roots of grass and trees planted on hillsides help to hold soil in place and reduce erosion.

FIGURE 8

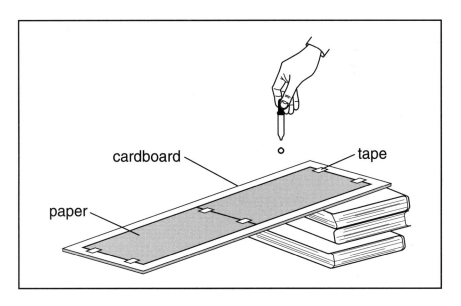

How does an incline affect a raindrop's splash pattern?

Experiment *1.9

ACID RAIN

To do this experiment you will need:

✔ **pH test paper and standard scale**

✔ **plastic containers**

✔ **rainwater**

Many of the gases that pollute the atmosphere dissolve in cloud droplets and fall to the earth as acid rain. The strength of acids is measured in terms of pH. Neutral substances, such as pure water, have a pH of 7.0. Substances with a pH less than 7.0 are said to be acidic. Substances with a pH greater than 7.0 are alkaline.

Many people don't realize that almost all rain is slightly acidic. In fact, it is quite normal to find rain with a pH as low as 5.6. That is why acid rain is defined as rainwater that has a pH less than 5.6. Acid rain can cause the pH of water in ponds, lakes, and streams to fall to a level that kills the eggs and seeds of various animals and plants.

To find the pH of rainwater, you can collect rain in plastic containers and test it with pH paper. By comparing the color of the pH test paper dipped in rainwater with a standard found on the container that holds the test paper, you can determine the pH of the rainwater.

You will need to use test paper that can measure pH to at least ± 0.5. That is, the paper should be able to distinguish pH 4.5 from pH 4.0 or pH 5.0. If your school does not have such test paper, you can buy it from a science supply house or from a store that sells fish or swimming pool supplies.

Test rainwater for pH at different times during a storm. Does the pH change as the storm progresses?

Test rainwater for pH at different times of the year. Does the pH of rain change from season to season? Is pH related to where you live? That is, is the rain in some parts of the country or world more acidic than in other places? A reference source will help you to find out. Would you guess that snow is acidic? How can you find out?

Of all our natural resources,
water has become the most precious.
(Rachel Carson)

The mist and cloud will turn to rain,
The rain to mist and cloud again.
(Henry Wadsworth Longfellow)

2

CLOUDS AND RAIN

When warm, moist air rises, it expands and cools. The water vapor in the cool air begins to condense forming tiny water droplets. Billions and trillions of these tiny droplets make up the clouds you see in the sky.

Clouds that form when the moisture in cool, expanding air condenses are natural clouds. They have probably existed for almost as long as the earth. But today we see other clouds, clouds that are the result of a human presence on earth. One of the most common of these is the vapor trail left by jet airplanes. The water vapor coming from the engines' exhaust cools rapidly and condenses. The condensed droplets form the familiar jet trail "clouds" that mark the path of high-flying jet airplanes. In very dry air, these jet trails disappear very quickly. But in still, moist air they may persist for a long time. Of course, wind will break up the trails quickly.

Clouds and More Clouds

You have probably lived long enough to know that some clouds indicate rain, while others are commonly found on fair-weather days. Fluffy, white, cauliflower-like, distinctly-shaped clouds that resemble heaps of loose cotton are called fair-weather clouds. They are cumulus clouds, one of the three basic types of clouds. The other two are stratus and cirrus clouds. Stratus clouds usually cover the sky like gray blankets. At ground level, stratus clouds are called fog. Cirrus clouds are high, thin, wispy, feathery clouds. Sometimes they are called mare's tails because they resemble the long, thin hair found in a horse's tail.

Figures 9a–9c contain photographs of these three basic cloud types. Meteorologists break these three basic types of clouds into more subtle classifications. If you would like to learn to identify the many cloud types, you can buy a small guide book for clouds or study a book on meteorology.

FIGURE 9A

Stratus clouds

FIGURE 9B

Cirrus clouds

FIGURE 9C

Cumulus clouds

Experiment 2.1

A CLOUD CAUSED BY CHANGES IN TEMPERATURE

To do this experiment you will need:

- ✔ an ADULT
- ✔ mirror
- ✔ heavy piece of cardboard approximately 25 cm x 50 cm (10 in x 20 in)
- ✔ water
- ✔ stove
- ✔ tea kettle
- ✔ ice cubes
- ✔ small bowl or pie pan
- ✔ salt
- ✔ coffee mug
- ✔ flexible drinking straw

On a cold day, you may have "seen your breath." What you saw was water vapor, a normal part of the air you exhale, condensing into tiny droplets as it came in contact with the cold air. On other cold days, you may have looked in vain trying to "see your breath." After you do the experiments in this chapter, you may be able to explain why you can see your breath on some cold days but not on others. In this experiment, you will begin by using your breath to form the particles that make up a cloud, even in the absence of cold air.

To see how the droplets in a cloud form, hold your open mouth close to a mirror and blow gently. The mirror becomes coated with a fine layer of tiny water droplets. In the same way, moisture condenses from air. As the air cools, water condenses forming the tiny droplets that make up a cloud.

To make a three-dimensional cloud, fold a heavy piece of cardboard about 25 cm (10 in) high by 50 cm (20 in) long, as shown in Figure 10. **ASK AN ADULT** to boil some water while you place a few ice cubes in a small bowl or pie pan. Add some salt to the ice to make it even colder. Place the bowl or pan on the folded cardboard as shown. **ASK THE ADULT** to place a mug half-filled with the hot water underneath the cold bowl. Can you see a cloud form where the hot, moist air touches the cold bowl?

To make the cloud bigger, **ASK THE ADULT** to use a flexible drinking straw to gently blow bubbles in the hot water. What effect does this have on the cloud that forms near the cold bowl?

FIGURE 10

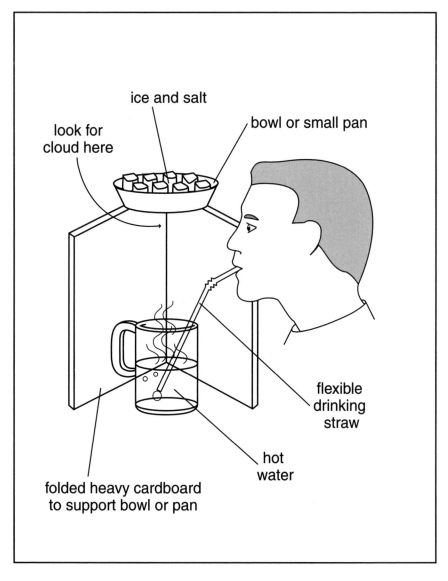

ice and salt

bowl or small pan

look for
cloud here

flexible
drinking
straw

hot
water

folded heavy cardboard
to support bowl or pan

You can make a cloud in your kitchen.

Experiment *2.2

A CLOUD CAUSED BY CHANGES IN PRESSURE

To do this experiment you will need:

- ✔ an ADULT
- ✔ 1-L or 2-L clear plastic soda bottle with screw-on cap
- ✔ cup
- ✔ water
- ✔ a friend
- ✔ flashlight or small lamp
- ✔ matches
- ✔ dark room

Remove the paper labels from a clear 1-L or 2-L plastic soda bottle. Pour about half a cup of water into the bottle, screw the cap back on, and shake the bottle vigorously for about 30 seconds. This should saturate the air in the bottle with moisture. Pour out all but about a tablespoon of water, and screw the cap back onto the bottle. Darken the room and ask a friend to shine a flashlight or a small lamp through the bottle while you squeeze the bottle with both hands (see Figure 11). By squeezing the bottle, you increase the pressure on the moist air inside. Now, release the bottle

FIGURE 11

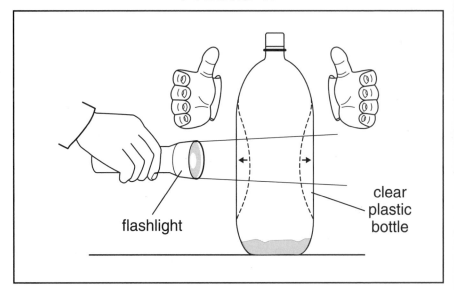

flashlight

clear
plastic
bottle

Does a cloud form when air pressure decreases, or is something else needed?

so that the pressure quickly decreases. Do you see any evidence of a cloud forming in the bottle?

Repeat the experiment, but before you screw the cap on for the second time, **ASK AN ADULT** to light a match, blow it out, and hold it inside the bottle so that smoke particles enter the bottle. If you have trouble getting smoke into the bottle, try squeezing the sides of the bottle before the match is lit. After the match is blown out and held near the mouth of the bottle, release the sides of the bottle. Air will enter the expanding bottle, dragging the smoke along with it.

Once you have gotten smoke into the bottle, screw the cap on securely. Shake the bottle again to be sure the air is saturated with moisture. Have your friend shine the light through the bottle while you squeeze the bottle and then suddenly release it. Do you see any evidence of a cloud forming in the bottle this time?

Clouds

As you have seen in the previous two experiments, clouds form when moist air cools or when air pressure decreases. However, there have to be small particles (nuclei) on which the water droplets can condense. In your experiment, those particles came from the smoke. Actually, when air pressure decreases, the expanding air cools. You have probably seen the opposite effect; when air pressure increases, the temperature of that air increases. That is why your bicycle pump becomes hot when you pump air into a tire. When you push the pump's piston into the cylinder and squeeze the air together forcing it into the tire, the air gets hotter. Some of that heat flows into the pump and you can feel its added warmth.

In the atmosphere, there are usually lots of tiny particles that can serve as nuclei for condensation. Particles of smoke, pollen, and tiny salt crystals from the oceans are usually present. As warm moist air rises into the atmosphere, the pressure at higher altitudes is usually less and so the air cools. The moisture in the cool, low-pressure air begins to condense on tiny nuclei. On a warm summer afternoon, you can see puffy, white cumulus clouds form. The moisture in the rising air cools and condenses, forming the tiny droplets that make up a cloud. Experiment 2.3 will show you why the warm air rises.

DID YOU KNOW. . .?

On the average, each cubic meter of air contains nearly 6,000 tiny grains of salt on which moisture can condense to form tiny droplets of water.

Experiment *2.3

WARM FLUIDS IN
COLD FLUIDS

To do this experiment you will need:

✔ thermometer, outdoor	✔ two small transparent glasses or vials
✔ small box	
✔ tape	✔ warm water
✔ cold water	✔ food coloring
	✔ eyedropper

Place a thermometer on the floor near the center of a closed room. To make sure no one steps on it, put the thermometer in a small open box. After about five minutes, record the temperature.

Next, place the thermometer near the ceiling. If there is no way to support the thermometer, ask permission to tape it to something near the ceiling. After about five minutes, read the thermometer. How does the temperature near the ceiling compare with the temperature near the floor? What does this tell you about warm air as compared with cold air?

A fluid is any material that takes the shape of the container in which it is placed. Both air (a gas) and water (a liquid) are fluids. Does warm water rise in cold water the way warm air rises above cold air?

To find out, place some cold water in a small transparent glass or vial. Put some warm water into another glass or vial. Color the warm water with a drop or two of food coloring. Stir the colored warm water. Use an eyedropper to remove some of the warm water. Place the end of the eyedropper down into the cold water and very gently squeeze the warm colored water into the clear cold water, as shown in Figure 12. Does the warm water rise or sink in the cold water? Does warm water in cold water behave like warm air in cold air?

Humidity and Dew Point

Moisture will condense from the air only if the temperature is at or below the dew point. The dew point is the temperature at which the air becomes saturated with moisture. Saturated means that the air holds as much moisture as it possibly can. Table 4 shows the greatest amount of water vapor that can be found in a cubic meter (cu m) of air at different temperatures.

FIGURE 12

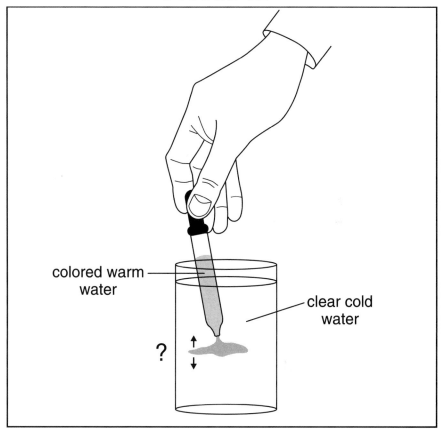

colored warm water

clear cold water

?

Will warm water rise or sink in cold water?

How can you use the graph in Figure 13 to determine the water vapor per cubic meter of air for temperatures that lie between, above, or below those in Table 4? As you can see from the table and graph, warm air can hold more water vapor than cold air. The amount of moisture that a cubic meter of air can hold at

TABLE 4

MAXIMUM AMOUNTS OF WATER VAPOR IN AIR AT DIFFERENT TEMPERATURES

Temperature (°C)	Temperature (°F)	Water Vapor (g/cu m)
0	32	4.8
5	41	6.8
10	50	9.3
15	59	12.7
20	68	17.1
25	77	22.8
30	86	30.0
35	95	39.2

a particular temperature is called the absolute humidity. Air at 30°C (86°F) can hold 30.0 g of water vapor before it is saturated. The absolute humidity of air at 30°C is, therefore, 30.0 g/cu m. If air at that temperature actually holds 15.0 g, we say the relative humidity of the air is 50 percent because it holds half the moisture it could hold. What is the relative humidity of air at 30°C if it actually contains 7.5 g of water vapor per cubic meter?

FIGURE 13

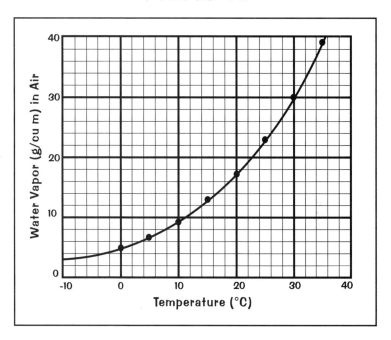

This graph shows the maximum amount of water vapor that can be found in one cubic meter of air at different temperatures.

How do we know how much water vapor the air actually contains? There are various ways that chemists can separate water vapor from the other gases in air saturated with water. By doing so, the amount of water that was dissolved in the air can be weighed. That is how the information in Table 4 was originally obtained. But once that table was available, it became much easier to determine the absolute and relative humidity of air. This is done by finding the dew point.

Experiment *2.4

MEASURING THE DEW POINT

To do this experiment you will need:

- ✔ warm water
- ✔ shiny metal can
- ✔ thermometer, outdoor
- ✔ pencil and paper
- ✔ small pieces of ice

You can determine the absolute and relative humidity of the air by finding the dew point. The dew point is the temperature at which moisture begins to condense from the air. You have probably noticed that you often find moisture on the outside of a glass that contains cold milk or soda. The moisture comes from water vapor in the warm air that condenses when the air comes in contact with the cold glass.

Suppose that you have a glass that contains water at 20°C (68°F). If you cool the water by adding ice, you may find that moisture (dew) begins to collect on the glass when the temperature of the water reaches 10°C (50°F). Since water is condensing on the glass, it must mean the air in contact with the glass became saturated when the temperature reached

10°C. From Table 4, we know that at 10°C the absolute humidity of the air is 9.3 g/cu m. At 20°C, the air could hold as much as 17.1 g. Therefore, the air holds only a fraction of the moisture it could hold at 20°C. That fraction is 9.3 ÷ 17.1. The relative humidity then is 9.3 ÷ 17.1 = 0.54 = 54%.

To determine the dew point of the air in a room or outdoors on a warm day, pour some warm water into a shiny metal can. Place a thermometer in the water and stir the liquid. When the liquid in the thermometer stops moving, record the temperature of the water. Then add a small piece of ice to the water and continue to stir as you watch the side of the shiny can. Continue to stir and add small pieces of ice to the water until you see tiny droplets of moisture condensing on the can. At the moment you see the droplets, read the thermometer and record the temperature. That temperature is the dew point. Use the dew point to find the relative humidity.

Repeat this experiment on different days and at different times of the year. How is the dew point affected by the weather? During which season of the year is the dew point temperature lowest in your home or school? During which season is the dew point temperature highest?

Experiment *2.5

THE LEAKING CAN THEORY

To do this experiment you will need:

- ✔ warm water
- ✔ shiny metal can
- ✔ other materials as needed

Suppose someone believes that the moisture on the shiny can is caused by water leaking through the cold can and not by water in the air condensing on the outside of the can. Design one or more experiments to show that the water does not leak through the can.

There's a silver lining
Through the dark cloud shining.
(Lena Guilbert Ford)

My heart leaps up when I behold
A rainbow in the sky.

(William Wordsworth)

3

RAIN AND COLOR

One of the most beautiful sights associated with rain is the appearance of a rainbow. Of course, not every rainy day has a rainbow. For a rainbow to appear, there must be both rain and sunlight. Furthermore, the sun must be fairly low in the sky. To see a rainbow, stand with your back to the sun and look approximately 40 degrees above the horizon (about halfway between the horizon and the area of sky directly above your head). You will see the sunlight reflected to your eyes from the falling raindrops. If the sun is very bright, you may be able to see a second, fainter rainbow about 10 degrees above the first one. If you look closely, you can see that the order of the colors in the second rainbow [violet (top), blue, green, yellow, orange, red (bottom)] are the reverse of those in the brighter one.

DID YOU KNOW. . .?

Despite the legend about a pot of gold at the end of a rainbow, there really is no such pot there. The people who know this for sure are those who have observed a rainbow from an airplane high above the earth. From there you can see that a rainbow has no end. It actually forms a complete circle. If you are standing on the ground, the bottom half of the rainbow is below the horizon.

Experiment *3.1

A RAINBOW IN YOUR YARD

To do this experiment you will need:

✔ garden hose   ✔ sunlight
✔ a friend

On a sunny day, you can make a rainbow in your yard. Turn a garden hose nozzle until it produces a fine spray. Have a friend hold the nozzle spraying the water up into the air while you look at the falling drops with your back to the sun. You should be able to see a beautiful rainbow in the sunlight reflected from the tiny water drops to your eyes. Which color is at the top of this rainbow? Which color is at the bottom? Can you see a second, fainter rainbow above the first one? If you can see a second rainbow, which color is at the top of this rainbow? Which color is at the bottom? After you have watched the rainbow for a while, let your friend enjoy the colors while you hold the hose.

Experiment 3.2

A RAINBOW FROM A PRISM

To do this experiment you will need:

- ✔ glass or plastic prism
- ✔ sunlight
- ✔ a friend
- ✔ white paper
- ✔ tape
- ✔ cardboard
- ✔ mirror

If you have a glass or plastic prism, take it to the sunny side of your house. Hold the prism between the sun and the house. **DO NOT LOOK AT THE SUN! IT CAN DAMAGE YOUR EYES!** Turn the prism, being careful not to shade it with your hand, until you see a partial rainbow (spectrum) on the side of your house (Figure 14). Have a friend hold a sheet of white paper taped to a piece of cardboard between the prism and the spectrum on the house. Can you see the spectrum on the paper? How do the colors in this spectrum compare with those in a natural rainbow? Can your friend use a mirror to reflect the beam of colored light onto the side of the house?

FIGURE 14

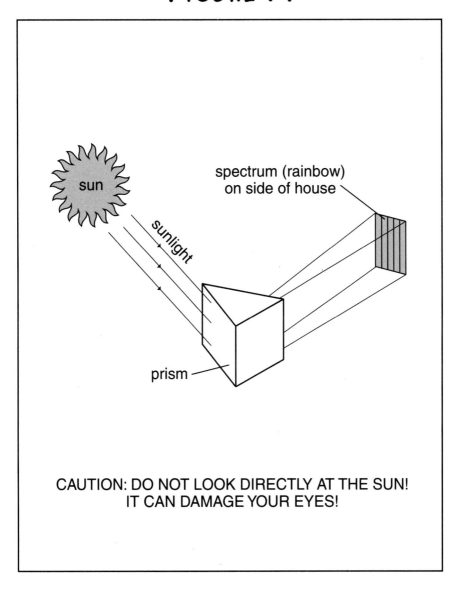

You can make a partial rainbow by holding a prism in sunlight.

Experiment *3.3

A Dark Room Rainbow

To do this experiment you will need:

- ✔ white paper
- ✔ glass of water
- ✔ table
- ✔ flashlight

Place a glass of water at the edge of a table. Shine a flashlight at a sharp angle down through the water, as shown in Figure 15. Move a sheet of white paper around beneath and to one side of the glass until you "capture" a rainbow on the paper. How do the colors in this dark room rainbow compare with those in a natural rainbow?

DID YOU KNOW. . .?

If you mix red and green light beams by shining both lights on a wall, the area where the beams overlap will be yellow.

Figure 15

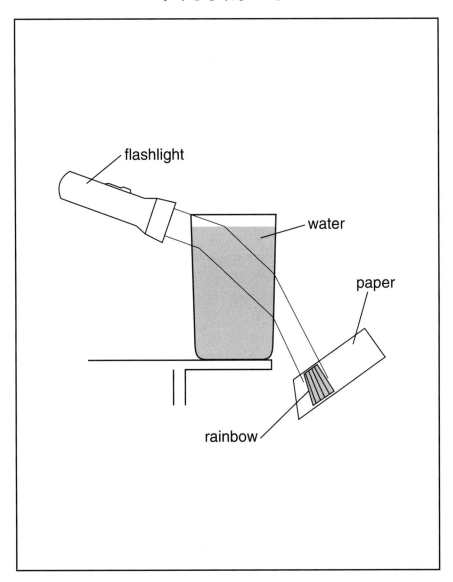

Using a flashlight and a glass of water, you can make a rainbow in a dark room.

Experiment 3.4

A BRIGHT ROOM RAINBOW

To do this experiment you will need:

- ✔ sunlight
- ✔ water
- ✔ mirror
- ✔ clear, shallow, rectangular glass or plastic container
- ✔ window

In this experiment, you will make a rainbow using sunlight, water (the natural ingredient of raindrops), and a mirror. Place a clear, shallow, rectangular glass or plastic container in a room so that it rests in sunlight streaming through a window. Nearly fill the container with water. Then place a mirror in the water. One end of the mirror can rest on the edge of the container. The other end should be under the water and resting on the bottom of the container so that the mirror is at an angle to the water surface and the sunlight, as shown in Figure 16.

The light will be bent (refracted) and separated into colors as it enters the water, just as it was when it passed through a prism. It will then be reflected by the mirror, as it

FIGURE 16

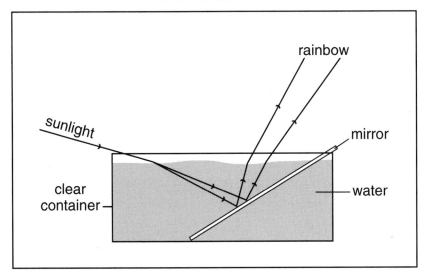

You can make a rainbow by reflecting sunlight after it has been refracted by water. The reflected light will be refracted again when it leaves the water on its way to forming a rainbow on the wall or ceiling.

may have been in Experiment 3.2. As the light leaves the water, it will be bent again and the colors further separated. The refraction and reflection of the sunlight by the water and mirror should produce one or more partial rainbows (spectra) that you see on the wall and/or ceiling. Perhaps, you can also see a bright reflected white beam of light. How can you show that this white light beam comes from light reflected by the unsubmerged portion of the mirror?

Experiment 3.5

LIGHT REFLECTED IN A RAINDROP

To do this experiment you will need:

- ✔ eyedropper
- ✔ water
- ✔ paper clip
- ✔ light bulb
- ✔ round-bottom (Florence) flask or brandy glass

If you have ever looked at the surface of a quiet pond, you know that light can be reflected by water. To see the light reflected from a drop of water such as a raindrop, use an eyedropper to place a drop of water on a bent paper clip, as shown in Figure 17a. Hold the drop about a meter (yard) to one side of a light bulb (Figure 17b). Look for images of the bulb reflected from both the front and rear surfaces of the drop. If you have trouble seeing these small images, try using a much larger "drop." You can make such a drop by filling a round-bottom flask (Florence flask) or a brandy glass

FIGURE 17

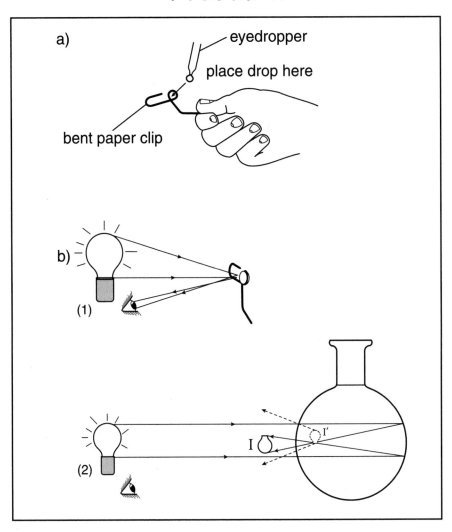

a) A water-drop mirror with curved reflecting surfaces can be made by placing a drop of water on a bent paper clip.

b) Look for light reflected from the drop (1), or from a larger "drop" in a round flask or brandy glass (2). You should be able to see an upside-down image, I, reflected from the rear surface of the drop and an upright image, I', reflected from the front surface.

with water. Hold this large drop about a meter (yard) to one side of a light bulb. Can you see images of the bulb reflected from the front and rear surfaces of the big drop? What do you notice about the images reflected from the rear surface of the drop?

DID YOU KNOW. . .?

Light bends (refracts) when it enters or leaves water. Look at a pencil in a glass of water. Notice how it appears to be "broken" at the water surface. To get a fish's view of the world as seen by refracted light, look at people sitting on the side of a swimming pool when you are underwater in the same pool. Try to explain what you see.

Experiment 3.6

LIGHT REFRACTED IN A RAINDROP

To do this experiment you will need:

- ✔ water
- ✔ light bulb
- ✔ eyedropper
- ✔ white file card
- ✔ paper clip

- ✔ magnifying glass
- ✔ magazine with fine print
- ✔ round-bottom (Florence) flask or brandy glass

You have seen that light is bent (refracted) when it enters water or glass at an angle. The change in the light's path cannot be the same for all colors. You know this is true because of the experiments you have done. You have seen that it is only after the path of a light beam is bent by water or glass that the colors in the light appear. As you saw in Experiment 3.2, violet light is separated from the other colors in white light because it is bent more than other colors in the light. Red light is separated because it is bent less than the other colors in white light. The difference in the amount that different colors in white light are bent accounts for the various rainbows you have seen, including nature's own true rainbow.

In a natural rainbow, light must be both refracted and reflected by the raindrops. To see that a raindrop can refract light, as well as reflect it, you will need water, a light bulb, an eyedropper, a white file card, a paper clip and a magnifying glass.

You can show that a raindrop can bend light just as a glass or plastic lens can. First, place a single light bulb on one side of an otherwise dark or dimly lighted room. Stand on the other side of the room and hold a magnifying glass (lens) in front of a white file card. Move the lens back and forth, closer to and farther from the card until you see a clear image of the light bulb on the card. Is the image of the light bulb right side up or upside down?

Figure 18a shows how the lens must have bent the light in order to form the image you saw on the white card. You can also use the same lens to magnify the print in this book. Place the lens on the print. Look through the lens and raise it toward your eye until you can see the image of the print clearly. Figure 18b shows how the lens bends light to form a magnified image. The light rays from the object that pass through the lens are bent so

FIGURE 18

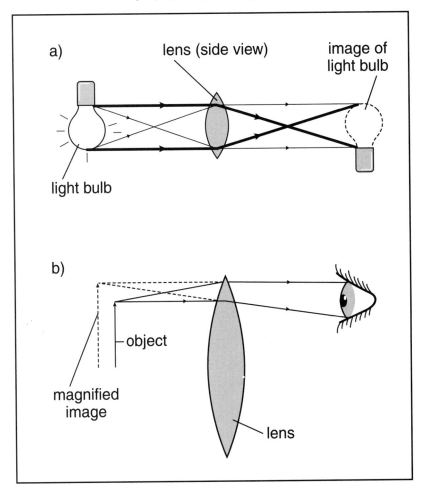

a) To form an image on a white card, the lens must bend the light as shown.

b) To form an upright, magnified image, the lens is held near the object. The drawing shows how the lens bends the light to form a magnified image. The dotted lines show where refracted light rays going to the eye appear to come from.

that they appear to come from an enlarged image.

Now repeat the experiment, this time with a water lens. Make a raindrop lens by using an eyedropper to place a drop of water on a bent paper clip, as shown in Figure 19. Hold the raindrop lens close to some fine print in a magazine resting in bright light. Even though you may be able to see only one letter or part of one letter through the lens, you will be able to tell that it is magnified. As you can see, the water-drop lens magnifies the print, just as a glass lens does.

Natural Rainbows

Now that you have seen how water can both reflect and refract light, you can understand how a rainbow is formed by raindrops. Some of the sunlight entering a raindrop near its top is bent, reflected off the back surface, and then refracted (bent) again as it emerges from the lower front of the drop. Because light of different colors is bent by different amounts, the colors are separated when the light is refracted as it enters and leaves a raindrop. In Figure 20a, only two rays of colored light—red (R) and violet (V)—are shown. These two colors, as you know, are at

FIGURE 19

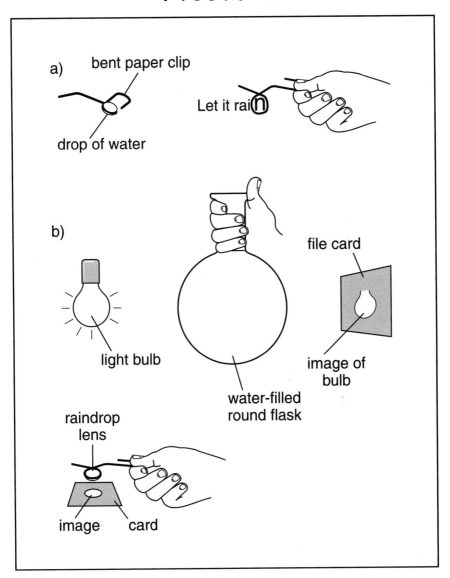

a) A water-drop lens is made by placing a drop of water on a bent paper clip. The water drop can be used to magnify print.

b) Use the same lens to "capture" an image of a light bulb on a file card. You can make a larger "water-drop" lens by using a round water-filled flask or a brandy glass.

the edges of the multicolored rainbow. They mark the limits of our color vision. There are other colors, such as ultraviolet and infrared, but we cannot see them.

At point A, where the sunlight shown in Figure 20a is refracted, some light, not shown in the drawing, is reflected from the surface of the drop. At point X, where light is shown being reflected back into the drop, some light is refracted as it passes through the drop. The inside of the drop is not a perfect mirror; some light passes through water and is refracted. Again, at point B where the light is shown being refracted as it reenters the air, some of the light striking point B is reflected back into the drop.

The fainter secondary rainbow is caused by sunlight that enters the lower front of a raindrop at C, as shown in Figure 20b. This light is also separated into different colors (shown here as R and V) when it is refracted upon entering the drop. The light that we see as the secondary rainbow is reflected twice inside the drops, at Y and Z, before it is refracted again as it emerges from the upper front portion of the raindrop at D. Of course, at each point where the light is reflected, some light is also refracted as it reenters the air. And at points C and D, where light is refracted, some light (not shown) is reflected.

FIGURE 20

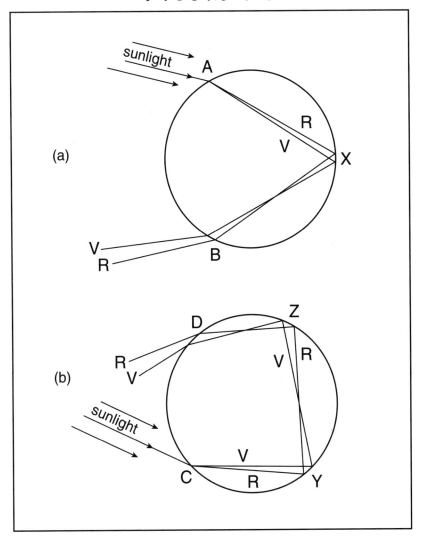

Sunlight is shown entering raindrops where it is refracted and reflected. The different colors in white light are refracted by different amounts causing the colors to separate.

a) Light is refracted at A and B and reflected at X. The light emerging from this drop forms part of the primary rainbow.

b) Light is refracted at C and D and reflected twice (at Y and Z). Light emerging from this drop is part of the secondary rainbow.

The diagrams in Figure 20 show how the violet and red rays of light are reflected and refracted to an observer's eyes by a raindrop. But, as you can see from the drawing, the red and blue light leave the drop at different angles. Only one of the rays (R or V, but not both) would reach the observer's eyes. The red that we see in a rainbow must come from different drops than the violet and other colors that we see.

In Figure 21, you see that a rainbow is made by an arc of falling raindrops. The red light in a primary (brighter) rainbow comes to us from the drops along its outer edge. The violet light comes from drops along its inner edge. The colors in between red and violet reach us from drops that lie between the edges of the rainbow. For the violet light, the angle between the observer and the light rays that we see coming to our eyes from the arc of falling raindrops is 40 degrees. For the red light, the angle is 42 degrees.

In the case of the secondary (dimmer) rainbow, the angle from the observer to the violet light is 54 degrees; for the red light, the angle is 50 degrees. For both rainbows, the spectrum of colors along the two arcs will continue to reach our eyes as long as the sun shines and falling raindrops continue to

FIGURE 21

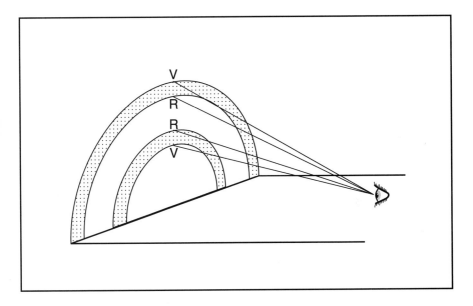

A rainbow is made from an arc of falling raindrops.

replace those that have fallen below the rainbows' arcs.

Other Colors from Rain in the Sky

Rainbows caused by moonlight reflected from falling raindrops also occur. With your back to a full moon on one side of the sky, you may see a faint rainbow if rain is falling from the opposite side of the sky. Such rainbows, called lunar bows, are dim and, generally, only the red to yellow portion of the bow is bright enough to be visible.

Halos are seen quite frequently. They are faint rainbow-like rings around the sun or moon. They are caused by light refracted from tiny ice crystals in high cirrus clouds. The ice acts like tiny prisms spreading the sunlight or moonlight into a spectrum. Often a double halo is seen, the brighter, inner one at an angle of 22 degrees and the outer one at 46 degrees. Because the crystals are turned at various angles, the colors are mixed, but usually the inner portion of the ring has a reddish tint.

Sometimes when the sun or moon shines through a thin fog, you may see a colored ring with the sun or moon at its center. This is caused by light diffracting (spreading out) around the fog droplets. This corona, as it is called, is easily distinguished from a halo. Unlike a halo which is reddish around its inside, the red in a corona is around its outside.

"Sun dogs" or "mock suns" are fairly common in polar regions. They also are seen in other regions when the sun is close to the horizon because of time of day or time of year. They are part of the halos described earlier.

They are much brighter than the rest of the halo and lie to either side of the sun. Their brightness is due to the fact that the ice crystals in the cirrus clouds that cause sun dogs reflect, as well as refract, a lot of sunlight.

God loves an idle rainbow
No less than laboring seas.

(Ralph Hodgson)

Oh! the snow, the beautiful snow,
Filling the sky and the earth below.
(John Whitaker Watson)

4

SNOWFLAKES: CRYSTALS FROM THE CLOUDS

When the air is very cold, the water droplets that make up clouds may freeze, forming tiny crystals of ice. These crystals collide with one another to form snowflakes. As the snowflakes grow, they begin to fall. If the air below is above freezing, the snowflakes melt and reach the ground as cold rain. But if the air is below the freezing point, the flakes will retain their crystalline structure and fall as snow.

But snow, like rain, does not fall evenly on the earth's surface. Some places, where freezing temperatures are rare, such as Miami, Florida, never see snow. The snowfall in Syracuse, New York in 1993 was 5,410 mm (213 in). During the same winter, at approximately the same latitude, only 241 mm (9.5 in) of snow fell in Portland, Oregon. In 1994, 3,200 mm (126 in) of snow dropped onto Syracuse, while only 102 mm (4 in) fell in Portland. Clearly, snow does not fall evenly in terms of space or time.

If a snow storm is accompanied by winds of 56 kph (35 mph) or more and visibility is reduced to less than 4/10 km (1/4 mi) for at least three hours, the storm is defined as a blizzard. One of the worst blizzards in history occurred during the four-day period of March 11–14, 1888. The famous blizzard of '88 blanketed the northeastern United States, caused 400 deaths, and left New York City buried in 6-m (20-ft) drifts. In January, 1952, a blizzard that piled up 15-m (50-ft) drifts near the Donner Pass in California's mountains left a City of San Francisco passenger train stalled in snow. Three days passed before rescue crews could reach the 226 passengers and crew.

Experiment *4.1

MEASURING SNOWFALL

To do this experiment you will need:

- ✔ ruler or meterstick (yardstick)
- ✔ sticks
- ✔ snow
- ✔ shovel
- ✔ paper and pencil
- ✔ large container with straight sides and narrow transparent container with straight sides used in Experiment 1.1

Unless the wind blows as the snow falls, it is easy to measure a snowfall. All you have to do is go to an open area and stick a ruler or meterstick straight down into the snow until it reaches the ground. The level of the snow on the ruler indicates the number of millimeters or inches of snowfall. If you mark this area with sticks, you can shovel away the snow and return to the same place to measure the next snowfall.

If the wind blows the snow into drifts, it is more difficult to measure snowfall accurately. You will have to measure the depth of the snow in a number of different places and find the average depth. You can do this by adding all the depths you measure and then dividing the sum by the number of measurements.

Total precipitation is measured as millimeters (or inches) of rain. To convert the depth of new-fallen snow into millimeters (or inches) of rain, fill the tall can or container you used to collect rain in Experiment 1.1 with the loose snow. Be careful not to pack the snow into the container. Bring the can inside and let the snow melt. As soon as all the snow has melted, pour the liquid into the narrower container you used to measure rainfall in Experiment 1.1. How many millimeters (or inches) of precipitation fell?

From the depth of the can and the depth of the water that forms when the snow melted, you can find how many millimeters (or inches) of rain would have fallen if the water had not frozen in the clouds. For example, if the snow in the can was 250 mm (10 in) deep and you found that the melted snow was equal to 12.5 mm (0.5 in) of rain, then you know that 250 mm (10 in) of the snowfall is equal to 12.5 mm (0.5 in) of rain. What depth of this snowfall would be required to produce 25 mm (1 in) of rain?

Collect samples of snow from different storms throughout the winter. Is the amount of snow needed to produce 25 mm (1 in) of rain always the same or does it vary with the type of snow? Does a foot of loose, dry, fluffy snow contain as much precipitation as a foot of heavy, wet snow?

Experiment *4.2

THE TEMPERATURE OF MELTING SNOW

To do this experiment you will need:

- ✔ large bucket
- ✔ snow
- ✔ cup
- ✔ thermometer, outdoor
- ✔ ice chest
- ✔ salt
- ✔ snow

Take a large bucket outside. Fill it with snow and bring it indoors. Scoop out a cupful of the snow. Place a thermometer in the cup and see what happens to the temperature. Stir the snow with the thermometer until the temperature stops falling. Does the temperature of the melting snow remain constant? What is the temperature of the melting snow?

What do you think is the temperature of the melting snow in the bucket? Place the thermometer in the big bucket of snow and stir the snow with the thermometer. Then read the thermometer. What is the temperature of the melting snow in the bucket?

Fill a large ice chest with snow and bring it inside. What do you think is the temperature of the snow melting in the ice chest? Use a thermometer to measure the temperature of the melting snow. What is the temperature of the big amount of snow melting in the ice chest? Was it the temperature you predicted? Does the temperature of melting snow depend on the amount of snow that is melting?

Pour some salt into a cup of melting snow. What happens to the temperature of melting snow when you add salt? Why do you think people throw salt on icy walks and roads?

DID YOU KNOW. . .?

Many substances melt at temperatures much lower than 0°C (32°F). For example, mercury melts at –39°C. What substance melts at the lowest temperature?

Experiment *4.3

EXAMINING SNOWFLAKES

To do this experiment you will need:

✔ magnifying glass	✔ warm jacket

You may have heard that snowflakes are hexagonal (six-sided) and that no two snowflakes are alike. You can look at snowflakes quite easily. Next time it snows, go outside with a magnifying glass in your jacket pocket. Allow some time for the outside of your clothing to become cold. Then let a few snowflakes fall on the sleeve of your jacket. Use the magnifier to look at the flakes. Because the warm air from your lungs will melt the snowflakes, you will have to hold your breath as you examine them.

Do the snowflakes look like the ones in Figure 22? Are they all hexagonal? Are any two the same?

When snowflakes first form, they are hexagons. However, as they fall they may bump into one another and break or stick together. If the air is warm, the crystals may

FIGURE 22

These are examples of some typically beautiful snowflakes.

melt or partially melt. As a result, snowflakes are often not the same when they land as they were when they first formed in a cloud.

Examine snowflakes from different storms and at different times during the same storm. Do the flakes from some storms have different characteristic shapes than those from another storm? Do flakes from the same storm change appearance as the storm progresses?

DID YOU KNOW. . .?

Blue Canyon, California, is the snowiest place in the United States. The average annual snowfall is 6.1 m (20 ft).

Experiment *4.4

MELTING SNOW FASTER

To do this experiment you will need:

- ✔ 10-cm x 10-cm (4-in x 4-in) squares of white, black, and various colored construction paper
- ✔ snow
- ✔ sunlight

On a calm clear day, place 10-cm x 10-cm (4-in x 4-in) squares of white, black, and various colored construction paper on top of some snow in sunlight. After a few hours, look at the squares. Under which square has more snow melted? How does this experiment help you to understand why you should wear dark clothing outside in the winter and white clothing in the summer?

One South American country spread black carbon dust over its mountain glaciers during the summer in an effort to increase its water supply. Why do you think they expected such a process would help to solve their water shortage?

KEEPING SNOW
FROM MELTING

To do this experiment you will need:

- ✔ snow or ice cubes
- ✔ insulated (Styrofoam) cups
- ✔ newspapers
- ✔ small boxes
- ✔ paper towels
- ✔ aluminum foil
- ✔ other insulating materials

Your house or apartment is probably insulated. This means the walls, ceilings, and floors are covered with materials that reduce the rate at which heat can escape in the winter and enter in the summer. Perhaps you can find ways to insulate a cup of snow and increase the time required for it to melt. You might ask your friends to enter a contest in which everyone is given a cupful of snow or an ice cube. The object of the contest is to see who can keep the snow or ice from completely melting for the longest time.

Of course, you will have to agree on some rules such as forbidding the placing of snow in refrigerators, freezers, and other cold places. You might want to supply some materials such as insulated (Styrofoam) cups, newspapers, small boxes, paper towels, aluminum foil, and other items that contestants may suggest.

Who can keep the snow or ice cube for the longest period? What methods were used to reduce melting? After contestants have a chance to discuss their various methods for keeping snow or ice from melting, you might hold a second contest. Are the contestants more successful in this second contest? Does the same person win for a second time or does a new winner emerge?

The horse knows the way
To carry the sleigh,
Through the white and drifted snow.
(Lydia Maria Child)

FURTHER READING

Asimov, Isaac. *How Did We Find Out About the Atmosphere.* New York: Walker, 1985.

Aylesworth, Thomas G. *Storm Alert: Understanding Weather Disasters.* New York: Messner, 1980.

Branley, Franklyn M. *It's Raining Cats and Dogs.* Boston: Houghton Mifflin, 1987.

Cosner, Shaaron. *Be Your Own Weather Forecaster.* New York: Messner, 1981.

Dickinson, Terence. *Exploring the Sky by Day.* Ontario: Camden House, 1988.

Gardner, Robert. *Water: The Life Sustaining Resource.* New York: Messner, 1982.

Gardner, Robert and Kemer, Eric. *Making and Using Scientific Models.* New York: Watts, 1993.

Gardner, Robert and Webster, David. *Science in Your Backyard.* New York: Messner, 1987.

———. *Science Projects About Weather.* Hillside, N.J.: Enslow, 1994.

LIST OF MATERIALS

A
aluminum foil
aquarium

B
baking flour
baking pan
  with cover
blackboard
books
bottle, clear
bowls
boxes, small
bucket, large

C
can, shiny
  metal
cardboard
chalk
cloth
clothespin
coffee can
coffee mug
coffee pot
concrete
  surface
containers
cups,
  Styrofoam

D
dish
distilled water
drinking straw

E
Epsom salt
eyedropper

F
fan
file cards
flashlight
flask, round-
  bottom
  (Florence)
food coloring
forceps

G
garden hose
glass, brandy
glass, drinking

H
hot plate

I
ice chest
ice cubes
ice, small
  pieces
insulating
  materials

J
jacket, warm

L
lamp, small
light bulb
liquid soap

M
magazine
magnifying
  glass
masking tape
matches
mirror
modeling clay

N
nail
newspapers
nylon stocking

P
paper
paper clip
paper towels
paper,
  construction
pencil
pie pan
Ping-Pong ball
plastic box
powdered
  sugar
prism

R
rain
rubber band
ruler

S
salt
sand or gravel
saucepan,
  glass
saucers
shovel
snow
soda

soil
sponge
sprinkling can
stake
stove
string
sunlight

T
table
tablespoon
tape
tea kettle
teaspoon
test tube
thermometer,
  outdoor

V
vacuum
  cleaner that
  will blow air
vial

W
warm room
water
waxed paper
window
wire
wood surface

Y
yardstick

INDEX